GOATs OF COLLEGE BASEBALL

BY WILL GRAVES

An Imprint of Abdo Publishing
abdobooks.com

abdobooks.com

Published by Abdo Publishing, a division of ABDO, PO Box 398166, Minneapolis, Minnesota 55439.

Printed in the United States of America, North Mankato, Minnesota.
102025
012026

Cover Photo: Jay Biggerstaff/Getty Images Sport/Getty Images
Interior Photos: University of Minnesota, 5; FSU Special Collections and Archives, 6; Wichita State Athletics, 9; Heinz Kluetmeier/Sports Illustrated/Getty Images, 10; Oklahoma State University, 13; Arizona State Athletics, 14; The Oklahoman/Imagn Images, 17; Ronald C. Modra/Getty Images Sport/Getty Images, 18; WSU Athletics, 21; UT Athletics Photo Collection/H. J. Lutcher Stark Center for Physical Culture and Sports, 22; LSU Athletics, 24–25; University of Tennessee Athletics, 26; MLB Photos/Getty Images, 29; Damian Strohmeyer/Sports Illustrated/Getty Images, 30; Matthew Sharpe/WireImage/Getty Images, 33; Steve Cannon/AP Images, 34; Donald Miralle/Getty Images Sport/Getty Images, 36–37; Larry Goren/Four Seam Images/AP Images, 38; Michael Reaves/Getty Images Sport/Getty Images, 41; Jonathan Mailhes/Cal Sport Media/ZUMA Press Wire/AP Images, 42

Editor: Dalton Rains
Series Designer: Kate Liestman

Library of Congress Control Number: 2025939139

Publisher's Cataloging-in-Publication Data

Names: Graves, Will, author.
Title: GOATS of college baseball / by Will Graves
Description: Minneapolis, Minnesota: Abdo Publishing, 2026 | Series: College GOATs: the greatest of all time | Includes online resources and index.
Identifiers: ISBN 9781098298302 (lib. bdg.) | ISBN 9798384932109 (ebook)
Subjects: LCSH: College sports--Juvenile literature. | Baseball--Juvenile literature. | Sports records--Juvenile literature. | College sports--Records--Juvenile literature.
Classification: DDC 796.35763--dc23

TABLE OF CONTENTS

DAVE WINFIELD

Dave Winfield's first love was baseball, but he couldn't be limited to just one sport. He also starred on the basketball team at Central High School in Saint Paul, Minnesota. Major League Baseball (MLB) teams already had an eye on the versatile athlete. After high school, he was drafted by the Baltimore Orioles. Winfield chose to stay close to home though. He arrived at the University of Minnesota in the early 1970s and soon brought his skills to both the baseball diamond and the basketball court.

Minnesota had been a college baseball power in the 1960s. The Golden Gophers won the College World Series in both 1960 and 1964. The multi-talented Winfield fit right in. He excelled as an outfielder. His blazing fastball made him the team's best pitcher. And he was just as dangerous as a hitter.

FAST FACT

Dave Winfield was such a great athlete that he was drafted by four different professional sports leagues. Besides baseball, Winfield was also drafted by teams from two basketball leagues. And even though he hadn't played college football, the Minnesota Vikings drafted him too. Winfield stuck with baseball. He made the MLB All-Star team 12 times and was elected to the Baseball Hall of Fame in 2001.

Winfield's best season came when he was a senior in 1973. He posted a 9–1 record with a 2.74 earned-run average (ERA) and 109 strikeouts over 82 innings. Meanwhile, he drove in 35 runs at the plate.

Minnesota reached the College World Series in Omaha, Nebraska, that spring. Winfield shut out Oklahoma for a 1–0 win in the first round. In the semifinals, he struck out 15 batters, keeping the University of Southern California (USC) scoreless for eight innings. The Trojans snatched a comeback win in the ninth, but Winfield was still named the tournament's Most Outstanding Player (MOP).

Minnesota's Dave Winfield batted .385 in 1973.

Florida State's Jeff Ledbetter earned national player of the year honors in 1982.

JEFF LEDBETTER

The left-handed Jeff Ledbetter did a little bit of everything at Florida State. When he wasn't playing at first base or in the outfield, he was an excellent pitcher for the Seminoles. However, he really thrived at the plate.

Growing up in Largo, Florida, Ledbetter hadn't been much of a power hitter. That changed in college. Florida State coaches helped the 6-foot-2-inch, 202-pound Ledbetter improve his decision-making skills at the plate. The guidance worked wonders.

Ledbetter regularly sent mighty blasts into the pine trees behind the right-field wall at Florida State's home stadium. In 1979, the freshman hit 13 homers. The next year, he hit 19. In 1981, Ledbetter sent 23 more into the pines. All those homers earned Ledbetter the nickname "Treetops."

Ledbetter saved his best for last. In 1982, the senior piled up 42 home runs. That set a National Collegiate Athletics Association (NCAA) record. No player had hit that many homers in one season.

Ledbetter said it sometimes felt as if he was using magic at the plate. The slugger created plenty of magic for the Seminoles. He left college with 97 career home runs, an NCAA record at the time. He also drove in a record-setting 346 runs during his time at Florida State.

PHIL STEPHENSON

From 1979 to 1982, Phil Stephenson spent four seasons rewriting the Wichita State Shockers' record books. A crafty and patient left-handed hitter, Stephenson was tough to get out. He almost always found a way to get on base. Stephenson knew how to wait for the right pitch. And his hitting form was close to perfect. He put together a 47-game hitting streak as a junior in 1981, breaking the NCAA record of 45.

Stephenson was so good he didn't have to crush the ball to get on base. The hit that extended his streak to 46 games was a short flare that plopped down just out of reach of the defense's gloves. It was just one more of Stephenson's NCAA-record 418 total hits. Stephenson was just as dangerous on the base paths as he was at the plate. In 1982, he set an NCAA single-season record with 87 stolen bases.

The most famous play of Stephenson's career wasn't a hit or a stolen base, but an out. Playing Miami in the 1982 College World Series, he found himself on the wrong side of a "hidden ball" trick. Stephenson took a few steps away from first base as he got ready to run to second. Then the Hurricanes' pitcher faked a throw to first. As Stephenson slid back, the first baseman acted as if the ball got past him and rolled into right field. Stephenson got up and took off to steal a base. That's when the pitcher actually threw the ball to the second baseman, who tagged Stephenson for the easy out. Miami went on to win the national championship. The fake throw became one of the most memorable plays in College World Series history.

Phil Stephenson posted an NCAA-record 206 stolen bases for his career.

WILL CLARK

When Will Clark was still in high school, he drove to Starkville, Mississippi, to visit with the head coach of Mississippi State's baseball team. The high schooler told the coach he wanted to be a Bulldog. In the end, Clark didn't become just any Bulldog. He became one of the best players in college baseball history.

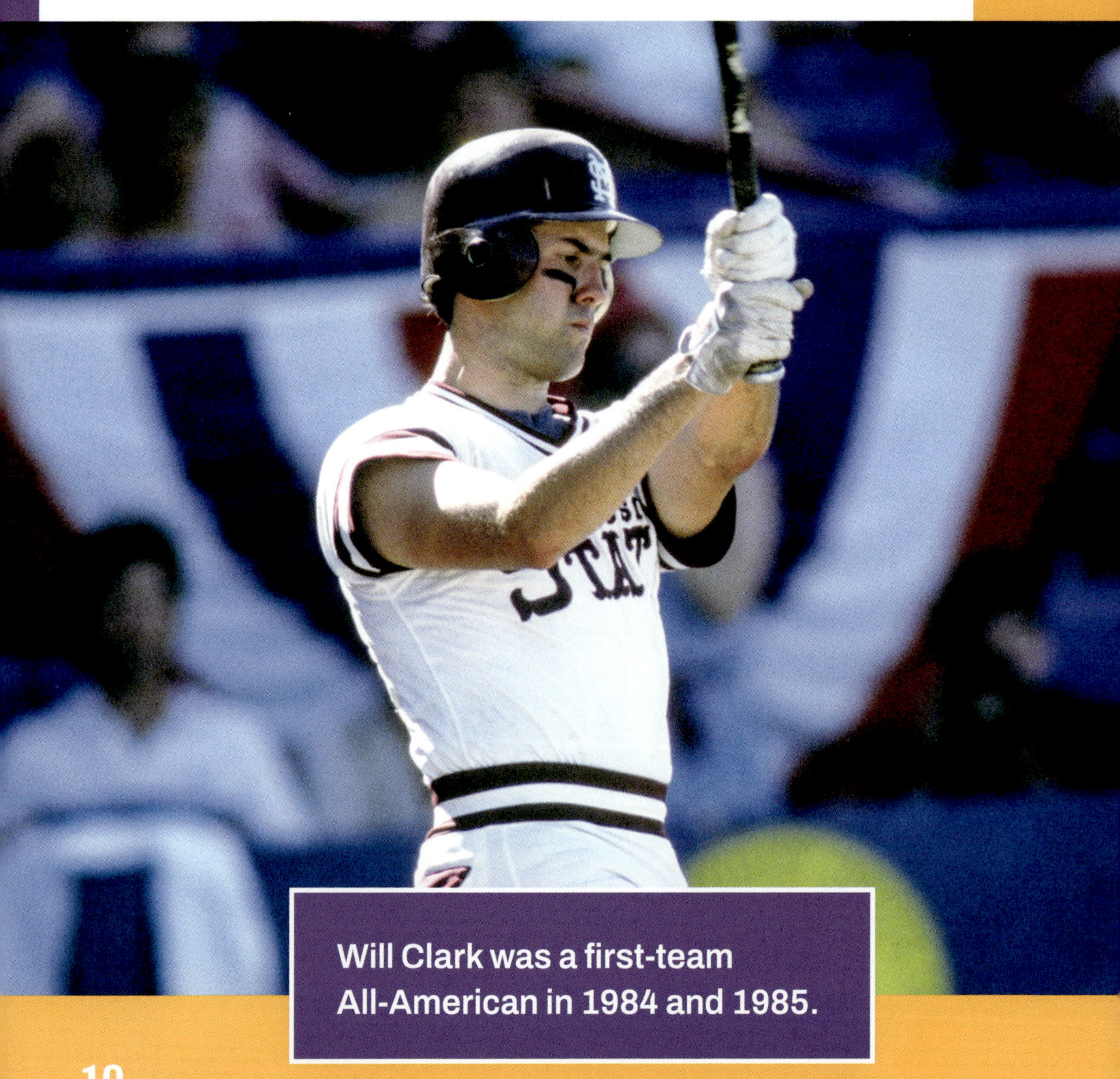

Will Clark was a first-team All-American in 1984 and 1985.

The first baseman, known as Will "The Thrill," spent three years delighting Mississippi State fans. He worked hard on and off the field. Before games, Clark would study tape of opposing pitchers, hoping to find an edge. All that research paid off. Clark hit an amazing .391 for his career, setting an NCAA record.

In 1985, the senior won the Golden Spikes Award, given to the best player in the country. That year, Clark batted .425. He recorded 25 home runs and drove in 77 runs for the Bulldogs. Clark also became the first baseball player to be named the Southeastern Conference (SEC) Male Athlete of the Year. He beat out Bo Jackson, a two-sport superstar in football and baseball from Auburn, for the honor.

Mississippi State thrived thanks to Clark and teammate Rafael Palmeiro. The duo, known as "Thunder and Lightning," powered the Bulldogs to victory after victory. Mississippi State reached the College World Series in 1985. The Bulldogs failed to win the championship, but not because of Clark. He hit .467 with a homer and five runs batted in (RBIs) in the tournament.

FAST FACT

During the summer after his junior year, Clark played for the US national baseball team. He showed his skills on the world stage at the 1984 Olympics in Los Angeles, California. Clark hit three home runs to help lift the squad to a silver medal.

PETE INCAVIGLIA

Pete Incaviglia's home runs didn't just scrape past the fence. The Oklahoma State slugger sent rockets over the outfield. He once smashed a homer straight into a scoreboard, causing a power failure.

Incaviglia didn't fit the mold of a typical star baseball player. He wasn't a naturally gifted athlete, his scruffy face always seemed to need a shave, and he joked around with his teammates a lot. Incaviglia was serious when it came to baseball though. The outfielder known as "Inky" dedicated 30 to 45 minutes each day to practicing his swing. During his three years with the Cowboys in the 1980s, he tried to turn every game into a Home Run Derby.

Incaviglia became one of the best power hitters in NCAA baseball history. He piled up 23 home runs in his freshman season. That would be a career best for most college players. It turned out to be Inky's worst season. As a sophomore, Incaviglia raised his season total to 29 homers. Then, as a junior, he blasted an NCAA-record 48 over the fence. That put him at 100 home runs for his career, setting another NCAA record.

With Incaviglia launching homers, Oklahoma State was a college baseball powerhouse. The Cowboys reached the College World Series during each of Incaviglia's three seasons. The slugger's record-setting output in 1985 remains one of the most impressive offensive seasons in NCAA history.

Oklahoma State's Pete Incaviglia earned national player of the year honors in 1985.

Arizona State's Barry Bonds posted a .347 career batting average.

BARRY BONDS

Barry Bonds almost didn't end up at Arizona State. The son of an MLB All-Star, Bonds was a top prospect. The San Francisco Giants selected the swift outfielder in the second round of the 1982 MLB Draft. But Bonds wanted a bigger contract than the Giants would offer. So he chose to play for the Sun Devils instead.

It did not take long for Bonds to prove he was one of the best players in the country. In 1983, he set the program's record for home runs by a freshman, smashing 11 over the fence. That record stood for 35 years. Bonds made the 1983 all-conference team too. However, his best was yet to come.

During his sophomore year, Bonds hit .357 and stole 30 bases while leading Arizona State to the 1984 College World Series. The slugger thrived on college baseball's biggest stage. He tied an NCAA record by registering seven consecutive hits in the tournament.

Before his junior year, Bonds decided he needed to tap into his power. He worked closely with an assistant coach to figure out how to put the ball over the fence more often. After another 11-homer season as a sophomore, Bonds found his groove as a junior. He drilled 23 home runs and was named to the all-conference team for a third straight year. Bonds finished his college career with 45 home runs and 175 RBIs. Having proved his talents at Arizona State, Bonds finally made the move to the majors. He went on to become one of the most accomplished MLB hitters of all time.

ROBIN VENTURA

Oklahoma State was the only college to offer Robin Ventura a baseball scholarship. The infielder quickly repaid the trust. Ventura was a hitting machine for the Cowboys during the late 1980s. When he swung the bat, the ball usually found its way to green grass instead of a fielder's glove. In 1986, the freshman's 96 RBIs were the most in the NCAA. And he was just getting started.

In 1987, Ventura was focused on helping Oklahoma State win games. He had no idea he was making history too. It wasn't until he had recorded a hit in 30 straight games that Ventura's Oklahoma State teammates told him he was on a tear. With each passing game, the attention around the hitting streak grew. The pressure didn't slow down the consistent hitter though. He built the streak up to 58 games.

Oklahoma State faced Stanford in the 1987 College World Series title game. Ventura's final at-bat of the game ended with a sharp ground ball to second base. The Stanford fielder stopped the ball but threw wide of first base. Fans wanted the scorer to rule it a hit. But it was an error instead, which meant Ventura's streak came to an end.

FAST FACT

Joe DiMaggio set an MLB record with his 56-game hitting streak in 1941. Ventura's streak went two games longer, and even the MLB great was impressed. DiMaggio said no matter what league you were in, getting a hit in 58 straight games was hard.

Still, Ventura had proven that he was one of college baseball's all-time greats. In 1988, he went on to win the Golden Spikes Award and the Dick Howser Trophy, which also honors the best player of the year. He was named to the College Baseball Hall of Fame in 2006.

Oklahoma State's Robin Ventura posted a career 329 hits.

Ben McDonald left college with 894 strikeouts in 198 starts.

BEN McDONALD

Standing at a towering 6-foot-7, Ben McDonald began his college career playing both basketball and baseball. The Baton Rouge, Louisiana, native arrived at Louisiana State University (LSU) in 1986. After striking out 144 batters as a sophomore, he turned his attention to baseball full-time. The right-handed pitcher rocketed to stardom thanks to a fastball that reached 98 miles per hour (158 km/h).

In 1989, McDonald began his final season with the Tigers by tossing 44 2/3 scoreless innings in a row. That set an SEC record that stood for 15 years. By the end of the season, McDonald had struck out a total of 202 hitters, another conference record. He also won the Golden Spikes Award.

McDonald mastered several pitches. His fastballs zipped past hitters and into the strike zone. When he wasn't overpowering hitters, he was outthinking them. His curveballs arced away from the bat. His changeup kept them on edge.

In 1989, the Tigers needed to beat mighty Texas A&M twice to reach the College World Series. McDonald pitched seven innings in the first game. He didn't go to the bench after coming off the mound though. He played the rest of the game in left field. LSU won 13–5. McDonald wasn't done. In the next game, LSU's coach called him up to the mound in the 11th inning. McDonald forced a ground ball to third for the final out of the game. LSU pulled off a 5–4 upset.

JOHN OLERUD

Early in John Olerud's career at Washington State, it seemed as if nothing could stop him. The first baseman and pitcher made a splash as a sophomore in 1988. He hit .464 with 23 home runs at the plate. Olerud was even better on the mound. The left-hander didn't lose a game all year, going 15–0. He was the first player in college history with 20 home runs as a batter and 15 wins as a pitcher.

Things changed the next winter. Olerud noticed a strange pain in his head. A short time later he fainted after a team run. Doctors put Olerud through a string of tests. They discovered a swollen blood vessel in his brain. If it burst, it could be deadly. Olerud had surgery to repair the blood vessel. He lost 20 pounds while recovering. When he returned, he wore a plastic batting helmet to protect his head on the field. Even though Olerud missed half the season, he still found a way to hit .359 and post a 3–2 record for the Cougars.

FAST FACT

Olerud made a lasting impression on college baseball. Every year, the College Sports Foundation gives out the John Olerud Award. It goes to the best two-way player in the NCAA. In baseball, two-way players perform as both pitchers and position players.

John Olerud posted a 26–4 record as a pitcher.

BROOKS KIESCHNICK

Baseball legend Babe Ruth was known for blasting towering homers. That wasn't all he did though. Early in his career, Ruth was also one of the best pitchers in the majors. As a kid, Brooks Kieschnick idolized "The Babe." He eventually excelled both at the plate and as a pitcher during his time at the University of Texas.

Brooks Kieschnick was a three-time first-team All-American with Texas.

The Longhorns were already a national power when Kieschnick joined them in 1991. He helped take them to the next level. Kieschnick was named the Freshman of the Year by *Baseball America* magazine after hitting 14 home runs and posting 66 RBIs. He was just as fearsome on the mound. The two-way star posted a 7–1 record as a pitcher. At one point, he tossed 34 straight scoreless innings, just two innings shy of a Texas record.

Kieschnick was just getting started. As a sophomore, he led the Longhorns in wins and shutouts. He gained national attention when he won the 1992 Dick Howser Trophy. Winning that award once is enough for most players, but not for Kieschnick. In 1993, he became the only player to win two Dick Howser Trophies. Kieschnick finished his college career with 43 home runs and 34 wins on the mound. The University of Texas retired Kieschnick's No. 23 in 2009.

FAST FACT

Kieschnick was a relentless competitor. He did whatever he could to help his team win. During the 1993 College World Series, Kieschnick threw 172 pitches in a game against Oklahoma State. Despite the workload, he took the mound again just two days later.

TODD WALKER

Growing up in Louisiana, Todd Walker dreamed of playing for LSU. A clutch home run in a high school state championship game helped him make that dream a reality. The huge hit helped him catch the attention of LSU coaches.

The 6-foot-tall Walker quickly succeeded at the college stage. In 1992, the infielder hit .400 with 12 home runs and 76 RBIs. *Baseball America* named him National Freshman of the Year.

Walker's early success set the stage for what was to come. As a sophomore, he led LSU to 53 wins and a berth in the 1993 College World Series. In the semifinals, the Tigers faced Long Beach State. They found themselves in a tight spot, down two runs in the bottom of the ninth. A few clutch hits tied up the game. Then Walker came up to the plate. The slugger hit a single into right field. It drove in the winning run for LSU.

The Tigers rolled to the championship game, where they faced Wichita State. Walker hit his third homer of the College World Series, and the Tigers cruised to victory. He was named tournament MOP for his dominant performance.

The championship only added to Walker's accomplishments. He finished his three seasons at LSU with a .396 batting average. He recorded 52 home runs, 246 RBIs, and 52 stolen bases. With those numbers, it was no surprise when the College Baseball Hall of Fame came calling in 2009.

Todd Walker was a two-time first-team All-American.

Todd Helton was named to the NCAA All-Tournament team in 1994 and 1995.

TODD HELTON

Todd Helton stayed busy at the University of Tennessee. During his first three years of college, he played both football and baseball. Sometimes Helton would practice both sports in the same day.

As a junior, Helton took over the starting quarterback job. However, an injury sidelined him after just three games. Tennessee fans weren't disappointed for long though. Helton was replaced by freshman Peyton Manning, who became one of the greatest quarterbacks in NCAA history. Meanwhile, Helton decided to focus on baseball full-time. He soon became a legend in his own right.

As a pitcher, the left-handed Helton threw strike after strike. He piled up 12 saves in 1995. He also led the SEC with a 1.66 ERA. Helton was just as talented at the plate that year. He could hit for average and for power, boasting a .407 batting average and an SEC-leading 20 home runs. Helton's play lifted Tennessee to the College World Series. He pitched an entire game in the first round, allowing just four hits. The Volunteers ended up finishing third, but Helton still won the Dick Howser Trophy that year as the best college player in the country.

FAST FACT

As a kid, Helton would practice his swing in his family's garage. All that practice paid off in college, and later in the major leagues. After a 17-year career with the Colorado Rockies, Helton was inducted into the Baseball Hall of Fame in 2024.

RICKIE WEEKS

Rickie Weeks didn't get much attention in high school. But then an MLB scout showed up to watch one of his games. The scout had come to watch another player. He left raving about Weeks instead. The scout's report helped Weeks earn a scholarship to Southern University, a Historically Black College and University (HBCU) in Louisiana. Southern already had a proud baseball tradition, and Weeks helped take the Jaguars to new heights. In 2001, the freshman center fielder recorded a .422 batting average. He also piled up 70 RBIs.

Still, not everyone paid attention. After the season, many of the nation's best players hoped to be selected for the US Collegiate National Team. When Weeks did not receive an invitation to try out, Southern's head coach called to complain. He thought Weeks wasn't getting attention because he played for an HBCU. The coach told the Team USA director that Weeks was good enough to play with anyone. The director gave in and offered Weeks a chance. A short time later, the director called back to apologize to the coach. Weeks wasn't just good enough to play on the team. He was outplaying nearly everyone.

Back in college, Weeks averaged .495 at the plate during his sophomore year. That earned him the NCAA batting title. He was even better as a junior. Weeks's .500 batting average made him the first player to win back-to-back NCAA batting titles. His .465 career batting average set an NCAA record too. Weeks also led Southern to the 2003 NCAA Tournament. In the regional round, he hit a three-run homer to lift Southern to a 5–3 victory. After the season, he became the first player from an HBCU to win the Golden Spikes Award.

Southern University's Rickie Weeks posted an NCAA-record .465 career batting average.

HUSTON STREET

Huston Street was raised by a University of Texas legend. His father, James, was a star quarterback who had led the Longhorns football team to a national title in 1969. When Huston arrived on campus in 2002, the freshman pitcher had big shoes to fill.

Huston Street piled up a Texas-record 41 saves.

Street was still a teenager when he became a closer for the Longhorns. Despite his young age, Street had the important task of protecting leads late in games. Closers must thrive in high-pressure situations. No player seemed to enjoy those moments more than Street.

Despite a unique windup, Street was a very consistent pitcher. His pitches always came out just the way he wanted them. But his greatest strength was his mental toughness. When he entered a game, he didn't think about the fans. He didn't think about the stakes, either. He just focused on making the right pitch. Other Longhorns players learned to relax when they saw Street jog out to the mound. They trusted their hard-throwing teammate to find a way to hold on for a victory.

The Longhorns cruised to the 2002 College World Series. Street appeared in three games during the tournament. He allowed just one run. In a title game matchup against South Carolina, he retired all five batters he faced. The young pitcher earned the save and locked down a national title for the Longhorns. Voters honored Street by making him the rare freshman to win the tournament's MOP award.

By the time Street moved to the pros in 2005, he was a Texas hero just like his dad. The pitcher piled up a program-record 41 saves. His 1.31 ERA was second-best in Longhorns history. And his five career saves in the College World Series was an NCAA record.

DAVID PRICE

David Price's path to baseball greatness almost ended before it began. The left-handed pitcher struggled during his freshman year at Vanderbilt. After a 2005 scrimmage, Price was so frustrated that he decided to quit. It took a long talk with his coach to change his mind.

The coach turned out to be right. Vanderbilt wasn't known as a baseball power when Price arrived. But over the next three years, that changed. Price helped the Commodores become one of the best programs in the country.

Price had a record-setting sophomore season. He struck out 155 hitters that year. No other Vanderbilt pitcher had done that. However, the record stood for only one year. Price broke it as a junior. He took out 194 hitters on the way to an 11–1 pitching record for the 2007 season.

Price used three different pitches to keep batters guessing. He loved to work deep into games, throwing at least 120 pitches in eight of his final 13 starts. In one 2007 game, Price pitched a full nine innings. He piled up a whopping 17 strikeouts along the way.

By the end of his college career, Price's early struggles were long gone. He became one of the most decorated pitchers in college baseball history. After his junior year, he won both the Dick Howser Trophy and the Golden Spikes Award. The Tampa Bay Rays thought so highly of Price that they selected him with the first-overall pick in the 2007 MLB Draft.

David Price posted a 2.63 ERA in 2007.

Buster Posey finished his career with 206 RBIs.

BUSTER POSEY

When Buster Posey arrived at Florida State in 2006, coaches expected him to pitch and play shortstop. He might even move to first or third. They didn't know how much more he could do.

Before Posey's sophomore year, Florida State's coaches asked him to play catcher. Posey agreed, and he quickly got to work. To get used to playing the new position, he would get into a catcher's crouch while watching TV.

By the end of his sophomore year, Posey was a finalist for the Johnny Bench Award, given to college baseball's top backstop. However, his workload behind the plate didn't slow him down as a batter. Posey's batting average went up from .346 in 2006 to .382 in 2007. He raised his RBIs from 48 to 65. As a junior, Posey was even better. He recorded a .463 average, with 26 homers and 93 RBIs. Posey claimed the Dick Howser Trophy, Golden Spikes Award, and Johnny Bench Award that year. When he moved on to the pros, he left behind a legacy as one of the best catchers in NCAA history. In 2019, the name of the Johnny Bench Award was changed to the Buster Posey Award in his honor.

FAST FACT

During one game in his junior season, Posey literally did everything. He fielded at all nine positions, using four different gloves. And he hit a grand slam to lift Florida State to a 10–0 win.

STEPHEN STRASBURG

Stephen Strasburg's right arm was ready for the big leagues when he came to San Diego State in 2007. It took some time for the rest of his 6-foot-4 frame to catch up. Strasburg spent his first year focusing on getting in shape and adding more muscle. As Strasburg grew stronger, his fastball got faster.

By the time Strasburg was a junior, his pitches topped 100 miles per hour (160 km/h). However, he could do more than just throw some serious heat. He had excellent control over his pitches. In three seasons at San Diego State, Posey struck out 375 batters. As a junior, he posted a 13–1 record with a 1.32 ERA. The next year, he set a program record by striking out 195 hitters. He threw a no-hitter in his final home game and led the Aztecs to their first NCAA Regional appearance in 18 years.

Strasburg wasn't just great against college players. He could hold his own against the pros too. He made the 2008 US Olympic baseball team, the first college player to make the team since pros were allowed to join in 2000. Strasburg helped Team USA win a bronze medal at the Games in Beijing, China. A year later, he was the top pick by the Washington Nationals in the MLB Draft.

Stephen Strasburg earned national pitcher of the year honors in 2009.

Kris Bryant recorded 62 RBIs in 2013.

KRIS BRYANT

When Kris Bryant hit his first Little League home run, his father gave him $100 as a reward. Later, Bryant's grandfather offered him $20 for every homer. If the practice had continued through Bryant's playing days at the University of San Diego, the slugger would have earned a lot of cash.

Bryant arrived at San Diego in 2011. That year, rules about the kinds of bats players could use became stricter. Hitting numbers fell all around the NCAA. The new rules didn't seem to slow Bryant down though. The 6-foot-5 third baseman spent his three seasons blasting home runs for the Toreros.

Bryant set a program record and led the nation with 31 homers during his junior year. That helped lift San Diego to a run in the NCAA tournament. For a team that hadn't seen much success, even a small run was impressive. After the season, Bryant claimed several honors, including the Dick Howser Trophy and the Golden Spikes Award.

FAST FACT

Bryant was selected by the Chicago Cubs second overall in the 2013 MLB Draft. He soon became one of baseball's top players. In 2016, he won the National League Most Valuable Player Award and helped the Cubs win their first World Series in over a century.

BRENDAN McKAY

From 2015 to 2017, Brendan McKay made two-way play look easy at Louisville. No matter the pressure, the pitcher and first baseman kept his emotions under control. He stayed so cool that it was tough to even get him to crack a smile during games. The left-hander from Western Pennsylvania was terrifying on the mound. He racked up 117 strikeouts and four saves as a freshman. He improved each season. By 2017, McKay struck out 146 batters and recorded a 2.23 ERA.

When McKay wasn't pitching, he was a fixture in the middle of the Louisville lineup. He hit .341 with 18 home runs and 57 RBIs in 2017. During a game against Eastern Kentucky, McKay tied a school record by hitting four home runs.

McKay helped Louisville become one of the best teams in the country. In an NCAA Tournament matchup against Kentucky, he threw nine strikeouts over seven innings. That clinched a spot for Louisville in the 2017 College World Series. There, he recorded his 11th win of the season against Texas A&M, hit a pair of doubles against Florida, and smashed a homer against Texas Christian University.

McKay finished his college pitching career with a 2.23 ERA and a program-record 391 strikeouts. At the plate, he added 28 homers and 132 RBIs. It was one of the greatest two-way careers in college baseball history. And McKay had the trophies to prove it. He won the Olerud Award as college baseball's best two-way player a record three times.

Brendan McKay earned national player of the year honors in 2017.

Paul Skenes posted a 13–2 record in 2023.

PAUL SKENES

Paul Skenes had a growth spurt late in high school. It pushed him from 5-foot-10 to 6-foot-6. Skenes took some time to figure out how to play in his bigger, stronger body. When he arrived at the Air Force Academy in 2021, he was more focused on becoming a fighter jet pilot than an MLB star.

Coaches had recruited Skenes as a catcher. However, the extra size had given him an extra boost of power at the mound. By the end of Skenes's sophomore season, his fastball was topping 100 miles per hour (160 km/h). He terrified opponents as the team's closing pitcher.

By then, Skenes was looking more and more like a future pro. Before his junior year, he transferred from Air Force to LSU. He hoped facing stronger competition in the SEC would better prepare him for the majors. However, Skenes didn't move his focus away from college just yet. He wanted to win an NCAA title. The pros would have to wait.

Skenes moved from the bullpen to the starting pitching rotation at LSU. He mowed down hitters all season. His 209 strikeouts set a single-season SEC record. Skenes cared more about wins than records though. The Tigers stormed to the 2023 College World Series. Their ace pitcher was at his best when the stakes were high. He made two starts at the College World Series, beating Tennessee and Wake Forest. His hard work paved the way for LSU to win its first national title since 2009.

HONORABLE MENTIONS

BOB HORNER

From 1976 to 1978, Horner whacked a school-record 56 home runs for Arizona State. The third baseman was named the College World Series Most Outstanding Player after leading the team to the 1977 title.

JOE CARTER

Carter slugged 58 home runs for Wichita State from 1979 to 1981. The outfielder's career .430 batting average set a school record and included an amazing .450 mark as a freshman.

GREG SWINDELL

Swindell, a left-handed pitcher, played at Texas from 1984 to 1986. He finished his career with a 43–8 record and 1.92 ERA. Swindell threw a pair of no-hitters and finished with 14 career shutouts.

DARREN DREIFORT

Dreifort pitched for Wichita State from 1991 to 1993. In 1993, he went 26–5 with a 2.24 ERA and 17 saves. He led the Shockers to a national title and won the Golden Spikes award.

JOHN POWELL

Powell played for Auburn from 1991 to 1994. The ace pitcher set an NCAA record by striking out 602 hitters over 477 innings. He lifted Auburn to the 1994 College World Series.

ALEX GORDON

Gordon was a dependable third baseman from 2003 to 2005. The career .355 hitter finished college with 171 straight games played for Nebraska. Gordon captured the Golden Spikes Award in 2005.

DUSTIN ACKLEY

A career .412 hitter, Ackley's 28 hits in the College World Series set an NCAA record. The first baseman led North Carolina in three straight College World Series appearances from 2007 to 2009.

GLOSSARY

batting title
The highest batting average in a season.

blood vessel
A tube that carries blood through the body.

clutch
Performing well in an important situation that often decides a competition or game.

conference
A group of schools that join together to create a league for their sports teams.

contract
An agreement to play for a certain team.

draft
A system that allows teams to acquire new players coming into a league.

earned-run average (ERA)
A statistic that measures the average number of earned runs that a pitcher gives up per nine innings.

error
A mistake in the field made by a baseball player.

recruited
Convinced a high school athlete to join a college team.

save
The job a relief pitcher does when he finishes a close game and secures a win.

scholarship
Money awarded to a student to pay for education expenses.

scout
A person whose job is to look for talented young players.

versatile
Able to perform many different roles or functions.

MORE INFORMATION

BOOKS

Buckley, James, Jr. *It's a Numbers Game: Baseball*. National Geographic, 2021.

Hustad, Douglas. *Innovations in Baseball*. Abdo, 2022.

Van, R. L. *Baseball: Then and Now*. Abdo, 2024.

ONLINE RESOURCES

To learn more about the GOATs of college baseball, please visit **abdobooklinks.com** or scan this QR code. These links are routinely monitored and updated to provide the most current information available.

INDEX

ABOUT THE AUTHOR

Will Graves has worked for more than two decades as a sports journalist. Since 2011, he has served as correspondent for the Associated Press in Pittsburgh, Pennsylvania, where he covers the NHL, the NFL, and MLB, as well as various Olympic sports.